<u>It's Time You Make A Change To Become A Better You!</u>

From **Eating Crumbs to Transforming WEALTH**

It's time to MOVE. LIVE. EXIST.

Parice Parker

Change Your Company – Change Your Season.

<u>*It's Time You Make A Change To Become A Better You!*</u>

From **Eating Crumbs to Transforming WEALTH**

Parice C. Parker

Change Your Company – Change Your Season.

It's Time You Make A Change To Become A Better You!

From Eating Crumbs to Transforming Wealth
Copyright © 2016 by Parice Parker. All rights reserved.

No part of this publication may be reproduced, stored in a retrieval system or transmitted in any way by any means, electronic, mechanical, photocopy, recording or otherwise without the prior permission of the author except as provided by USA copyright law.

Scripture quotations, unless otherwise indicated, are taken from the *Holy Bible, King James Version*, Cambridge, 1769. Used by permission. All rights reserved.

The opinions expressed by the author are not necessarily those of Fountain of Life Publisher's House.

Published by Fountain of Life Publisher's House

P. O. Box 922612, Norcross, GA 30010
Phone: 404-936-3989
Please Email Manuscripts to: publish@pariceparker.biz
For all book orders including wholesale email: sales@pariceparker.biz

Fountain of Life Publishing House is committed to excellence in the publishing industry. The Company reflects the philosophy established by the founder, based on Psalm 68:11, *"The Lord gave the word and great was the company of those who published it."*

Book design copyright © 2016 by Parice Parker. All rights reserved.
Cover Design by Parice Parker
Interior design by Phyllis R Brown
Editor: Phyllis R Brown

Published in the United States of America
Copyright Library of Congress
ISBN   978-0-9904441-6-9
Date: May 22, 2014

<u>*It's Time You Make A Change To Become A Better You!*</u>

From **Eating Crumbs to Transforming WEALTH**

This Book is Dedicated to:
Kent Crumpler & Lorraine Hopkins

We appreciate your love, prayers, and acts of kindness. Thank you for being our friends during the time of our purpose journey. You are the most humble and respectful people appointed in our lives during this season. It's an honor and a pleasure having the opportunity to know you. We could not imagine life without you.

Love,
The Parkers

Change Your Company – Change Your Season.

It's Time You Make A Change To Become A Better You!

From **Eating Crumbs to Transforming WEALTH**

A true visionary never dies they visualize.
                              ~Parice C. Parker

It's Time You Make A Change To Become A Better You!

From **Eating Crumbs to Transforming WEALTH**

Table of Contents

Dedication *5*
Introduction *8*
Preface *10*

Chapter

Company Matters *14*
View Points *35*
Revealing Points *49*
What's In Your Heart? *62*
Who Am I? *71*
Cultivate Your Ground *82*
Sweat & Get Results *93*
Running Power *104*

Parice c Parker

It's Time You Make A Change To Become A Better You!

From **Eating Crumbs to Transforming WEALTH**

Introduction

***O**ften* I have seen people with vision go nowhere, simply because the company they keep is negative and cannot inspire vision. What good is a visionary with gifts buried in the grave and what good is life without vision? Vision is life and once dead it will not work. Wealth comes through visionaries that execute on their vision and, as a result, they obtain great possessions. Make your life count and let your life be an inspiration to others. There comes a time when you must choose a better life, set a higher standard and anticipate ownership to a more prosperous life. The choice is yours. If things in your life are not coming together, then you must change the way you live and the company you keep? You have the power to decorate your life as you choose. Your resource is not where you are, but in your path forwardness and taking control of your destiny. Now is the perfect time to make a change from

It's Time You Make A Change To Become A Better You!

eating crumbs to transforming wealth by the way you live and changing the way you reflect life!

Parice C. Parker

It's Time You Make A Change To Become A Better You!

From **Eating Crumbs to Transforming WEALTH**

Preface:

The company you keep does matter. Whoever you associate with is a replica of your future, believe it or not. Your prosperity will be responsive with the company you keep; as the old saying goes, "birds of a feather flock together." Proclaim your new life through reforming the way you think and the company you keep. Yes, it does matter. Often lives will stay in the same condition because NOTHING and NO ONE is challenging them. The company you keep alters your season because your atmosphere begins to change. NO VISION requires NO WORK and wrong association yields No Good Results in Your Life!

Challenges are formulated to help one develop, grow, and mature. Is the company you're keeping causing intelligence in your life or do they have a smearing effect? A lot of people take good relationships for granted, and they do not miss them until they are gone.

It's Time You Make A Change To Become A Better You!

Allow people of good stature in your life because those are the ones that will help you develop to your full potential. Get Rid those that remove life from you.

Too many have stayed in the same predicaments decade after decade until it has become a natural part of their life. Living an abnormal life is never good for anyone especially your children. Get tired of eating crumbs and desire an entire feast of a more abundant life. A lot of people have forgotten how to live good and productive life. Many wonder why no change has come, but you have to think prosperity and be willing to be prosperous if you desire to receive prosperity. Prepare your inner treasures to surface because the power to transform wealth is buried inside you. Your wealth transfer does not require money, but endeavor to gain victory and the power to endure the birthing of your dreams. Proclaim your vision, unlock your wealth and transform your life.

Parice C. Parker

<u>*It's Time You Make A Change To Become A Better You!*</u>

From **Eating Crumbs to Transforming WEALTH**

A QUITTER will lose every time, but ONE THAT TRANSFORMS Always Defines SUCCESS.

~ *Parice C. Parker*

<u>*It's Time You Make A Change To Become A Better You!*</u>

From **Eating Crumbs to Transforming WEALTH**

Fountain of Life Publisher's House
<u>***www.pariceparker.biz***</u>

<u>*It's Time You Make A Change To Become A Better You!*</u>

From **Eating Crumbs to Transforming WEALTH**

Chapter One
Company Matters

Making up your mind is the most challenging thing in the world because it requires change. If you desire transformation, you must go after it with a made up mind. Failure is not an option, and what life is currently offering you is no longer acceptable. You cannot be the same because the truth is revealing vital points to your inner being that will anticipate this transformation to be evident. You could not comprehend that the company you kept mattered, but now you are willing to make all necessary changes. Get the best experience in relationships you can.

There is power in vision

There is power in vision and visionaries. I had this idea years ago of a women's group and for years, it was spoken into my life. It is The Remade Woman Global Network, and it impacts countless. Since I went forth in the vision, I have met beautiful people, and now I could not imagine my life without them. When you receive vision and operate in that thing you can visualize, it's life restoring. I met this one woman, Nellie Wuso, who is the author of The Keeper of Me. She is a phenomenal woman, speaker, business advisor, heart advocate, and friend and possesses a powerhouse character. The Remade Woman added definition to my life and many others such as my dear friend Reverend Phyllis R Brown, the author of The Superhighway. She is also a powerful woman that has brought great meaning to my life and edited things that needed to be corrected. Reverend Phyllis R Brown is a woman of distinction, class, an excellent example of a great teaching ability and so much more. The conversations we have shared are priceless. Yes, there is power in vision; that is why you must go forth with just a thought because, at this end, it will be made manifest. I did not think I could achieve but with the grace of the vision, The Remade Woman Global Network divinely connected us all. Our relationships were divinely connected through visualizing The Remade Woman Global Network. Get the best experience in relationships that you can. Better requires more to come out of you and develop a stronger mindset. You want new; it is simply just new. Change takes you out of your usual mindset and modifies your life. Often many have failed to realize the torment of their lives because they ignore the truth and are not willing to open their eyes. Yes, the truth just simply hurts. However, it possesses real transformations. Change is an eye opener, and it must take place for the instant replays to stop reoccurring in your life.

Vision open doors

I was a featured guest on Atlanta Live 57 in Norcross Georgia, and it was my third appearance. I met Psalmist Gina Redwood after the show. We were both on during live recordings and my husband gave the producer our card. Afterward, she called, and I asked if she would be our featured Psalmist. "Yes," she replied, and she sang with such anointing and passion. We all came together because of the vision, The Remade Woman Global Network "Discover the Virtue in You" tour. Afterward, a mark of unity was branded in our lives on May 31, 2013, along with Shawn Johnson the author of Rising Above Now, Minister Sonya Curtis, the author of Easier & Lighter and Sherly D. Allen the author of Walking Through Your Pain. As we all met during a conference call, we felt the power of togetherness as if we had known each other for life. Vision forms and causes a function to go forth and make life easier and better. The impact of a visionary and the potential of the vision is life changing.

It's Time You Make A Change To Become A Better You!

It reminds me of this woman that stood out as a particular vessel. I was lead spiritually to consider her for prayer, and she prayed. Wow, and a powerful prayer it was by Apostle Eva Grant. The Remade Woman Global Network created a new life for us all. Your vision has great potential, but you must maximize it. Your new friends are in your destiny call. A man without vision shall die, and your gifts will make room for you to great men and women plus doors of opportunity will be made available to you. Proverbs 18:16. Now, so much we all obtain during our coming together, and we all help sharpen each other's vision. Real vision is an efficient well that produces more to spring forth. Afterward, Annette Alexander and I conversed over the phone; she is the author of Faith Going In. We discussed some dynamic plans to be even more successful. The only way to break a cycle or curse is to change for the better and adjust the way you think. Once you transform the way you think a difference will be noticeable and change will be effective. You have the power to alter your season right now by the decisions you make and the way you think. Notice, change will always add or delete in your life. Which one do you prefer? It is your life, and you must live it. It is better to live a good and productive life than just to allow life to lead you; especially to places you do not want to go. Take control and choose the best life you can. Notice, everyone that is around you or comes into contact with you will be affected by your lifestyle! Your life is representing and inspiring good or bad. What style of life are you promoting? If you take a deep look at your life, would you want to relive it? If no, then what transformation are you causing to occur in others? How effective is your life? Would someone desire to become you? If you cannot change the way you think, then you cannot change your life. That is why change is so valuable and better decisions must be made. Transformation keeps us in a creative mode that causes greater challenges to become effective. The power to conquer ship is when you overcome. A visionary mind stays in a creative mode. Something is always being designed, and a plan is always being set. A visionary cannot perform without visions; they must see first then act afterward. A visionary was not born to fit in, or become a follower, But they are made for the purpose to accomplish greatly. Change cannot happen until your mind is made up to alter your new life season!

The Spinning Cycles of Your Life

Once a revelation comes to you, innovation will begin to motivate your mind to reform your thinking and modernize your decisions. Innovation solves problems. It is your creativeness that makes change happen. Transformation occurs once the rotation of nothingness continues to spin and your eyes are open now. Notice the things that are appealing to your eyes, it cranks up a shift to drive you forward. It further causes your heart to desire after it until the conversion has taken place. The problem most people face is they want to see a result, but never take the

It's Time You Make A Change To Become A Better You!

vision and desires severe enough to make things happen.

Change is crucial, and it possesses the solutions to your pursuit of happiness. Some things in your life you just have to make them exist, regardless of what you will go through. It must be achieved by any means necessary, and your determination is the pathway. Nothing from nothing leaves you with nothing. Give your mind something to see and your sense of reality something to feel that your confidence will ignite a greater spark in you. So many speak of tiredness, but are not willing to do anything about it! You must be prepared to make that change so that transformation will happen for you. Only you can make this decision.

Change Your Company – Change Your Season.

It's Time You Make A Change To Become A Better You!

A cycle is something that rotates and reoccurs whether it is good or bad. You have the choice to turn those unwanted cycles off and to stop them from spinning things around in your life. Changing circles with the company you keep will change your cycles! Turn your thinking around. Successful thinkers were not born with great wisdom; they all anticipated innovation and transformed.

The Keys to Your Heart Desires

The key to all your needs being fulfilled and your heart's desire coming to pass is to utilize your creativeness. Groundbreaking results are in your innovation. Creativity is to serve a purpose, and that is to fill a void or solve problems. Change causes us to advance in areas of lack or a state of insufficiency. It takes a moment to imagine all your problems are solved through your creativeness. Yes, the majority can happen, but you must anticipate it by cranking up your innovative mind. Surely if you socialize with negative people, they will keep strife, and envy and hostility stirred up in you. Hope will be in the opposite direction of your mind after you are feeling drained. Keeping your mind in a golden state is extremely vital. Whoever they are will soon be a result of your habitation. It will show forth what is in your mind? Nevertheless, if you are around good thinkers, they will manifest positive thinking in you. Sooner or later because of your relationships, you will begin to think and operate either negatively or positively. Yes, you hold the keys to your destiny and how your life ends up is dependent upon the choices you make. Your decisions give you the opportunity to turn things around in your life for better or worse. The choice is yours to receive the keys to your heart's desires or just have another dream of what if. Now, it is time to be sensible and make wiser decisions because your associations are the key to your life.

The Company You Keep Are Tools in Your Life

Believe it or not is the exact do not care attitude many have had towards their associations. A lot of people cannot improve their life because they have simply made poor choices; perhaps doing the right things, but with the wrong people. Being selfish or jealous will always keep one back. The company or relationships you keep are tools in your life that will either sharpen or dull your motivation. Also, the decisions you make will affect your present and alter your future.

I will never forget this one friend I had. She always made me laugh, and we had a lot of fun together. We talked and caused each other to think sharper. We had a lot in common and finally I figured I had found a true friend. Yes, we had known each other for years, but she did not have my best interests in mind. One day I opened my eyes and wondered whose benefiting the most out of this friendship? It was not me. I always kept her company and when she needed me I was there. However, others received greater recognition in their ministerial gifts than me. Often, I felt used and unappreciated. Moreover, I stopped what I was doing to be a listener when she needed to talk. I also realized she never came to any of my book signings; neither did she support the sentimental victories that inspired me. I have had strangers to encourage the best to get out of me and appreciate me more. Have you ever felt that way in the company of a friend or family member? Perhaps, they made you feel less than you are. If so, the relationship is not healthy because both should benefit equally.

One is using the other to bypass time. Value yourself more and you will stop allowing people to disrespect you. Are you not better than the love and respect they show you? Never expect others to care more about your change than you; because it will not happen until you get serious about the treasures that are inside you. Wealth is not something that cost money it is something that you must earn through your determined effort to seek.

The Crumb Associates

A crumb here and a crumb there just to keep you crawling for more and making sure you do not rise higher than them. These are the ones that have all you need to set you up but are not willing to invest or boost your change. Be extremely careful around these people because they can cause your change to take plenty of steps backward. That is their objective, to keep you in a rearward position while they broadcast all your bad news. These people possess serpent bites. You cannot see them hurting you because they are too busy scattering your fragments. A crumb here and a crumb there sooner or later bits and pieces are thrown everywhere. Now, you are too busy crawling around taking your mind off of rising to pick up fragments trying to survive. These people have kept you in a downward position with depression and distractions while back biting you all along. Leave those crumb droppers alone because they mean you absolutely no good.

Selfish & Jealous Associates

Rising with these kinds of friends and associates around is hard. They will deceive you. If they give you a little, then it will always keep you on the need for more. Selfish people will criticize you to keep you at the place you want out of, and they want you to accept it as good criticism. Speaking, they see you higher than you see yourself, but they are not willing to help you achieve your uprising. However, their true intentions are to keep you stationed just where you are. Also, if you recognize the power and zeal to you, then you will be much further ahead. If people cannot support your accomplishments or the innovations in you, then remove yourself. Relationships are a supportive bridge that should cause an improvement in your life. The company you keep matters especially if you are planning to achieve significant things in your life.

There was a moment in my life where I began to have it extremely hard. It was the toughest and most trying time of my life; I meant last time. Every time I attempted to

It's Time You Make A Change To Become A Better You!

look up all I saw was the bottom of the rock in my view. I did not know how I was coming out, but I knew I was coming out bigger and better. A few people I knew began to wonder and left my side. Your vision is never for another to push in a manner you will. Get serious enough to make your dreams materialize. Never get comfortable with the company you keep and always guard your heart. It's nice to get to know new associates because at times it will be the stranger that will encourage you more. The key is to continue in every effort of your life transformation. Your dreams are within it. Change is your number one priority, so you can gain a new life perspective. Anything that is in the need of correction for your life needs a life transformation.

It's Time You Make A Change To Become A Better You!

Assessment Check of Your Company

Make sure the company you keep cares about you and will promote the good in you to come out. Your daily attitude and character feed your mind good or bad. Your mind must be angled on rising every moment of your day to continue this great change. Every second count. One wrong move will delay your prosperity to change that is why it is so valuable to evaluate everyone in your life. If they are not on your side one hundred percent, they can cause a time lapse in your life transformation. Instead of forwardness, you will move many steps backward. Give absolutely no one that victory over your life change. Your life transformation is the outlook of this elevation. You need to set criteria to evaluate your associates. It is never easy changing, and you do not need anyone or anything holding up your progress. The viewpoint of your shift.

Assess your company. Notice their value for your life. If there is no value, they will serve you no purpose. No purpose and no meaning equal no good outcome. You do not need people taking up valuable space and quality time in your life or a day that you could be building a better life. Value your time and evaluate your change because it is the time you make a change.

It's Time You Make A Change To Become A Better You!

From **Eating Crumbs to Transforming WEALTH**

Chapter Two
View Points

Self-examination is the key point of this dynamic change in you. No one could desire it to happen to you. Your outcome portfolio must landscape your hope and cause your belief to know that you can. If you can paint the picture and see it then, your faith can cause it to be real. It is impossible to paint a picture you cannot grasp in your sight. Therefore, if you can view it then it is all possible! Get that spectacle of doubt out of your eye. There is no room for smearing vision. Write the vision and *make it plain. Observe your future because this vision must be in the big prospect of your destination.*

Open Your Eyes & See

The only reason you are not there yet is because you did not get serious enough for your heart's desire to be real. Open your eyes and what do you see? Complaining will not help you because it is negative and nothing good can come to pass until the complaints stop. You cannot look ahead if your mind is always in your past. Let go and live your life transformation. Look onward, you can work smarter and try harder. If you disagree with anything in your life, change it. You have the power to cause any change. Once self-inspection is over, then you can observe your present to think about a better future because your complaints will be over. The biggest problem you have ever had is you. Change begins in the heart and causes the way you think to re-modify so your life can transform. As you look toward your future, you will observe even more change. To become a better person your mind requires a new way of thinking. Consider a bigger you through inhabiting a bigger thinking capability. Expand your thoughts and get wiser through educating your mind in the things you did not know. Wisdom enriches the mind and gives knowledge on larger strategy. If your mind is not capable of becoming bigger than the obvious, then you will never reach your goals because goals will always surpass what and who you are now. Goals are formulated to cause you to stretch to a new height, aim for a higher level and take you to places you have never been, but you are destined to go. Quite naturally, it requires much more out of you!

Are You Thinking Too Big?

Big thinkers have big dreams and the bigger the dream, the bigger the challenges. Notice, the reason some people cannot dream big is because they cannot accept that it can be a reality. These are procrastinators and pretenders. A procrastinator is one that has what it takes but is not willing to step up to the plate and be bigger. A pretender does not put the time or the effort to grow the vision. They pretend to exist in greatness but are entirely opposite. Nevertheless, they will copy others to look like they are big and they mimic anyone that is different than them. Mimicking becomes so natural they do not recognize what they are doing. They are truly in denial to proving self because as long as they are pretending to be big or someone else they feel accomplished at fooling others. Sad to say, they take everything for granted and are not willing to grow up to the standpoint of their duties.

Procrastinators and pretender have a lot in common. The bigger the dreamer, the greater the hope and the more significant the effort! Thinking big causes your hope to be expanded, strengthened and stretched. You can no longer operate under your norm because you are required to become more major you!

If you have complaints too, file

A complaining spirit is never satisfied because it is never happy. Happiness is something we all must pursue and fight. The only way to delete a complaining spirit is come up with a solution to your problems. Simply put; you need a cure. As long as one is complaining they cannot become innovative and see ahead because their mind is too busy bickering about the past. It is vital to move forward because time is too precious to waste and the history has gotten you to your now season.

Complaints will sour your zeal to push, to press or to put forth the effort. It is time to put the past in the past and, if not, build a creative vision from it. Yes, it was my history that caused me to visualize so much. During many trying times in my life, I built something from it, from music to books and visions to business. It was during my terrible times that caused me to create good times through being determined not to face times such as those again. Get as far away from the bad and the lack. It is only you that can do whatever needs to be done for this prolific change!

A Change in the Atmosphere

If change is what you need to become a better you, then your atmosphere will be full of new hope. Visions are given to increase our knowledge of ourselves. You have reached your limits; now it is time to grow bigger. What used to satisfy you is no longer filling the gap? An urgency of expansion is filling your atmosphere, and that is causing your hope to see bigger. Change only exist where there is a gap that must be filled. Hurts and pains never feel good, but a lot of good comes from them. Many peoples' visions were built in their most difficult times. Eighty-five percent of businesses and fabulous ideas came from ones' hardship. Ideas solve problems! If there is not an issue, then a solution cannot be made or invented. Innovation will then be impossible. What and how can your problems be solved? That is the beginning of your creation to becoming a bigger you. Your problem solver is the start of your vision. What is it? Music was mine during the start of my growth to a bigger me. God gave me a song. I Need To Move On. That was the start of a talent I did not know I had. Although my mother is a great songwriter, I did not know I was. It was that moment of hurt that pierced my heart, and the way I bled was through music. At that time music gave me hope and soothed my pain. Some things in you are going to birth a bigger and better you. It is already inside, but you just have to figure it out. More significant you require a greater determination, one you have never known. Therefore, you need to get to know the new you.

Write the Vision

Writing vision requires a view point. What is in your perspective? The question is what do you see? Regardless, how crazy or far-fetched, it may still write the vision. Writing vision is not easy and sometimes, in the beginning, it does not make any sense.

It's Time You Make A Change To Become A Better You!

However, continue because it will require footwork, research, and a determined mind. Vision comes many different ways; through painful times, loss, struggles, stress, pressures, troubles, strife, and sickness. Over seventy-five percent of rich and wealthy people GAIN VISION TO GET OUT OF POVERTY! What if Wal-Mart stores DID NOT exist during our difficult times in the U. S. when our economic downfall occurred? Can you imagine the explosive rate of poverty, homelessness; unemployment and substance abuse would have been four times higher?

Sam Walton's vision greatly sustained and had a good impact on our economy with Wal-Mart stores. The vision of Sam Walton stores of Wal-Mart with 4,112 plus stores and more than 680,000 associates in 14 countries outside U. S. helped sustain countless family incomes. Now, what if Sam Walton would not have set aside the time nor made the effort to write his vision or had decided to quit? Vision building is a plan in progress, and an attempt determined not to fail. What if he would have limited his vision just to one store and not included Sam's wholesale? I admire his tenacity because he never stopped writing vision even though he is now deceased; his vision is still living and still growing. One store would have added to our great home and business foreclosure rate as well as increased our unemployment rate with well over 679,959 people. WOW, how much did his vision help our country? How many more knew that Sam Walton existed after the vision of Wal-Mart came into existence? There is more life once your vision prospers and the more prosperous it is, the more purpose you will serve. No one needs a problem, but problem solvers. Now, which one are you going to become a problem or a solution to the problem? People need visions that pertain to their needs and it is the time you become the supplier because suppliers are buyers. Leaders are the heads and not the tails.

Now, What Do You See?

I am chosen to show many viewpoints on standing for something and writing vision. My life assignment is to inspire the greater you to triumph. Feed your vision life through keeping your hope alive with a positive attitude. Never let any situation, circumstance or condition stop you from writing your vision. What may not work now may work later, but keep on writing.

Many laughed at me and did not believe that I survived eight strokes. My life purpose is to inspire countless people to become operable in their divine assignments. The enemy tried to destroy me so I could not exist as an inspirational author and get to you. I just decided that strokes were not going to have the best of me, but I was going to get the best out of my great afflictions. I begin Stroke Walk & Certified Stroke Survivors. A stroke prevention vision came from my sickness, and healthier people will survive. Always keep your mind on the good no matter how bad a situation may be. Let the good works abound from it. Get busy and be creative until your innovativeness solves your problem. Never stop writing

It's Time You Make A Change To Become A Better You!

because a vision always sees new hope and search new ways to stay thriving. A true visionary never dies they visualize. Now, what do you see?

It's Time You Make A Change To Become A Better You!

From Eating Crumbs to Transforming WEALTH

Chapter Three
Revealing Points

*M*any *do not like to admit their hurt and pains because they are too busy ignoring reality. The wounds of a failure will damage the hope of the vision. Too many people have put their visions on the back burner because they failed and lacked success. The lack of confidence caused the heart to be burdened with the, "I cannot" spirit. Eventually, I cannot spirit took hold of the vision and put the vision* *in a box. It is normal for an, "I cannot" spirit to stand up first in our minds before the I can spirit can be acknowledged. Your wealth and inheritance are in the unraveling treasure of your vision, but many begin putting effort into other venues to satisfy their needs of survival. Perhaps, a lot of people do not want to face the true challenge of becoming successful because of the intense requirements to be fruitful. A QUITTER will lose every time but ONE THAT TRANSFORMS Always Defines SUCCESS. Do not let I cannot overpower the I can. Keep I can in the front of your mind and you will!*

Trade in I Cannot for I Can

It is good to keep the right company because they have influence in your success. If you are unsuccessful in your dreams, it is because you have the wrong company in your presence. Company with bad spirits, negative attitudes that are non-inspirational do not have any hope and will depress your vision. You cannot bear good fruit out of the wrong company or be successful while you oppress. Good company always empowers and expects better of you because they too want to prosper. Today, trade in the I cannot spirit for the I can.

Working with Damaged Goods

Your goods need to perfect in the weak areas. There is nothing wrong with your wealth ideas; however, there is a problem with the abuse you allowed others to use to disrespect you. A lot of people put me down and laughed at my efforts, but I did not allow that to stop me. Though many times my heart was bruised I did not give up on my wealth ideas. Those ideas had all the potential to transforming wealth in my life. Yes, more than once I put my vision in boxes and put my attention in areas that were not causing me to overcome but survive. I allowed others to ignore me and cause me to get weary and neglect my vision. Get tired of surviving then you will begin to activate your conquering attitude. Once activated, everything becomes I can. Since you have not made it yet, get away from those that make your vision feel worthless and go in a new direction. You cannot look back because your greatest conquest is ahead and in a different direction from where you have been. Go forward and become new. Watch how effective your vision becomes when you change directions. Staying in the same area around the same people will damage and delay your vision. Too many have buried their wealth ideas because they gave up hope. No hope equals any success. Vision must remain hopeful. Get away from those that are killing your hope to transforming wealth. Your seed is depending on you.

Neglecting Your Vision Will Omit Your Needs

Keep in mind the wealth that is in your vision; not so much the money, but the prosperity that defines wealth. The irreplaceable moments cannot be purchased with cash, but with the pursuit of your happiness and freedom to live profitably. Cherish the moments of no more misfortunes.

It's Time You Make A Change To Become A Better You!

Wealth deals with noncash values, such as overlooking peace, hope, guarding belief and trust. Often dreams of your children or your heart' desires will be neglected because of your entire wealth ideas. Opportunities will miss because of your vision not being operable. You will miss out on big events, special occasions and good times all because you did not pursue your happiness and allow your wealth to transform. It is all in your vision that the wealth will transfer, and your life will change. Stop eating the crumbs off the table and feast on the right of your labor.

First, take all your wealth ideas out of the box and brush them off. Once you stop neglecting it, you will not miss out on any more valuable moments. What if you can take a weekend trip with your family without penny pinching? Close your eyes as your children ask you for gifts you can say, "Yes I can." As your spouse needs something you can say, "Yes I can." As the time comes around for that special occasion, you can say, "Yes I can." Notice, I can is treasured; it possesses your happiness and releases your pursuits.

Working with Damaged Hope

Damaged hope cannot move forward. It serves no good and produces no purpose. Broken words cause a lot of discomforts, and they will damage your hope. A lot of people have no confidence in accomplishing because the first thought is negative. Have you ever been put down so much it caused your spirit to be slothful? You must be extremely careful who you socialize with because all their words are powerful. Words possess the power to crank you up or cause you to break down and quit. The vitality of this equation is how long will it take you to crank back up and how much will you lose in the process of a breakdown? The frequent association will cause a positive energy flow that will positively impact your life.

I cannot do this will never accomplish, but I can achieve every goal and strives for perfection will cause an overflow. Acknowledgment identifies the successor and fear proclaims a failure. Once you remove yourself from damaged speakers, you will begin to see life come back to your vision. Know that your wealth transfer is inside of you so stop looking for it in others. As one writes the vision, it should speak to hearts, and people will begin to run with it. Speaking, promote it and help support. Progress is essential to be successful. So, therefore, your vision is not to be shared with anyone that has a destructive mindset, while it is in the making. Everyone cannot and will not receive your vision and are not happy for you or willing to help you to pursue it. If they are not for you, then they are against you.

Exchange the Damaged Attitude for New Hope

I Cannot Apologize For The Truth! If we as people have never come together, the time is now. We have built cities with our bare hands and have had great ideas. The only way we as people are going to rise is to recognize the power within! Many have overcome great obstacles and are willing to settle for less to get what they need. It is time to mark your territory and exchange the negatives for a new attitude. Are you not tired of your dreams and heart desires incarcerated, falling unemployment and depending on government subsidies? Put your priorities in order. Do not wonder who's going to support your vision keep moving ahead and go in a new direction.

Revealing Relationships

Relationships are stronger than you think. I mean all possessing power. People have life changing effects on your life. One way or another, the company you keep inspires your rising or falling. I remember one of my clients once told me she followed a friend up a flight of stairs, and that friend was her husband. Afterward, she got hooked on drugs. Many days she regretted going up that flight of stairs. It caused her to lose so much because she went the opposite of her dreams. Her loved one steered her in the wrong direction for many years and during those years her children and family suffered a massive loss. Be careful and beware of the company you keep because the path they are walking you will eventually follow.

Getting To Know The Real You

It is time to share your vision with people that keep you inspired. Prospectively as you empower, it keeps your vision in a possible position. Discussing your wealth ideas with non–visionaries can cause you terrible devastation in your spirit. Give no one the authority or opportunity to dismember your zeal, while your wealth ideas are in transformation. The more you are challenged is, the more you find out a little bit more about you. A new strength begins to surface. Challenges are our spiritual work out. They help keep us in mental shape. Many people are afraid to exchange their old way of thinking for the new, but to produce a better life; you must be transformed and renewed your mind to reach your full potential.

It's Time You Make A Change To Become A Better You!

From **Eating Crumbs to Transforming WEALTH**

Allow your no to become the fuel of your push.
~Parice Parker

It's Time You Make A Change To Become A Better You!

From **Eating Crumbs to Transforming WEALTH**

Chapter Four
What's In Your Heart?

When your days turn into night and your nights turn into nightmares, "What do you do?" So many feel they deserve a much better life and are no longer satisfied with life as it is. Most people are inspiring everyone to become better and they become more successful. Now it is time to put forth that same effort to increase your capabilities. It is time to take a deep look at you. I ask you this question. "What's in your heart?"

It's Time You Make A Change To Become A Better You!

Getting To Know You

Getting to know yourself is one of the most difficult things you will have ever to face. You have more personalities, let downs, excuses; negative attitudes than anyone remains in your company. The one person you can never run from is you. One person, you see every day is you. So it is required that you transform because you cannot run away from yourself. Transformation formulated through many different things in life. Life transformation is more during critical times or when one's zeal is cranked up to overdrive; forcing the old you to be more powerful, and then you will begin to operate in a new strength. You are the only one that could love you so much until a change takes place.

It's Time You Make A Change To Become A Better You!

Change Is Never Easy

I have counseled so many people in my lifetime to become greater. I was a cosmetologist for years and I was able to reach so many hearts. A lot of individuals listened to me and took the advice I gave them. For years I counseled them privately as I serviced their beauty needs, not realizing the impact I had in their lives. Some furthered their education, started new businesses to become more successful, but most of all transformed their wealth. Furthermore, all followed their heart. You must look into your heart and find out what can keep your heart in a healthy position. What causes it to beat? Notice, as heart beats there is life. So figure what is in your heart and give it life. Life changes things. Are you a life changer or do you need a change in your life? Transformation is never easy because the change must come from within. Now, it's time you become that which is in your heart. By any and all possible means persevere until you make that change happen.

New Identity

During transformation the old you will be exchanged for the new and it is a process. I know every day you look in the mirror and see a very familiar person looking back at you. Who are you? You saw things in you that no one else sees. You have noticed things about you that no one else is able. Who is that stranger looking back at me? You just cannot figure yourself out, even though you thought you knew. The transformation begins when you start noticing yourself change. You are no longer willing to be that person you used to be because you desire a change and deserve a better life. You know your past and it is nothing to relive again. Now, you are ready to know your tomorrow because you realize there is more hope ahead. God is identifying you to be greater? Your life has been scrutinized, your heart played with and your essence has went astray. Simply ask yourself the question. Who am I?

The Click

You have allowed the perception of so many people to make you appear less than what you are purposed to be. You have heard your cries, felt your tears and been victimized many times in your life. You have wrestled with yourself to be more. You have shared your deepest and darkest secrets with you. You have trusted you with your entire life and have ridden every thriller life roller coaster ride with you. And you cannot even get rid of you because for the rest of life you are stuck with yourself. You have tried to push you away, but you would not budge. Nevertheless, you have tried motivating yourself to do better, but you were discouraged. You know that person in the mirror deserves a far better life, and your dreams are worth living. You have seen how others have abused and used you. Too many have taken you for granted. You have done all you can to satisfy everyone else, and now it is simply time you appreciate you. One day I was sitting in church and as Bishop L D Parker preached about the 30, 60 and 100 fold; imme-

diately, I heard the voice of the Most High and the question was "What fold are you?" I know many people have heard the message about the seed sowing, but that day reality clicked on. A thought in my mind clicked and, reality forced my heart to motivate I am to exist. That day I begin to prepare as never before to raise the value of my life, so I can add more value to others. What fold are you? The fold represents your worth. Is your life value appreciating or depreciating, because one or the other is happening? Do something amazingly good to cause you to become a better you.

Give Your Life Definition

Your former life is now history and tell the old you goodbye. Get a new identification

It's Time You Make A Change To Become A Better You!

(I. D.). Your past has caused a new formula in your life and it is better than you ever had. The life you desire is breathtaking and your life will have a whole new definition. Life is a terrible thing to waste and a lot of people do it every day. I have been one in that number wasting valuable time, days and opportunity to increase my life. We all are found guilty of wasting time but it does not have to continue. Deficit occurs when value begins to depreciate or nothing is happening. Therefore, when loss happens in life it is because value has been lost somewhere. Value is priceless when one appreciates the interest of growing. Through the years many forget to be grateful for opportunity and that is why the loss is so devastating. You must take the time to appreciate opportunity to become all you can. Do not waste an-

other opportunity of reaping the benefit of a 100 fold cultivator. Simply ask yourself the question again, "Who am I?"

It's Time You Make A Change To Become A Better You!

From **Eating Crumbs to Transforming WEALTH**

Chapter Five
Who Am I

Questioning whatever people have characterized you as, take it off. Do not allow the words of others to put you in a box and put a label on your identity. Have more respect for yourself. Too many people let others classify them with a mark then it becomes their description. Wearing a label can have power over your destiny and being around people that disrespect you will consume your hope. A tag describes you and your name is irrelevant *because the label has categorized you. It is vital that you get to know who you are because then your identity will be revealed. You cannot show others who you are until you dig deeper. Getting to know who you really are will define your life and give you purpose to live. A lot of issues will be resolved and your tenacity will be driven to the point of your fulfillment. Put your target in your view and keep the pursuit of your purpose in your eyesight. Always be in preparation to excel and anticipate the day of your elevation. A true visionary is determined to excel and tarry to a have great victory. Visionaries also have continuous creative minds and they are always thinking innovation. A visionary strives until a visionary thrives. If you agree with your label regardless of what it is, wear it. However, exert yourself until you be-*

gin to flourish so that every label will be removed from you. Do not tell who you are. Show them!

The Hunt Is On

Wakeup call; now, the hunt is on! I was more than just a cosmetologist, but also a great aspiring author as well as a life motivator. If I would have never took that leap of faith you would not be reading this book. Notice, I just did not go from being a cosmetologist to an aspiring author and motivational speaker overnight. It took a greater me to accomplish this work and it took years to develop. I had to get more determined and hunt for the new me to exist. I was destined and determined to live a life of happiness.

It's Time You Make A Change To Become A Better You!

It was ironic every time I pictured my great grandfather Elliot Richard Culp Sr. and grandfather Elliot Richard Culp Jr. they were always laughing or smiling. I never saw a frown on their faces or sadness. More so than anything, they were always laughing. It is hard to find happy people, but in them it was natural. A life full of laughter is what we all should have and are destined to pursue. Sadness should be replaced with happiness and deleted from your vocabulary. Imagine everyone in your household always smiling, laughing, and happy. What an effect your household will have on others?

Myles Monroe's testimony encouraged me on how he was persistent to get a certain job. As he was going for an interview he did not meet all requirements to obtain the posi-

tion. A few others were waiting for an interview. Yes, they had degrees and higher education and would have more than likely been a better candidate, paper-wise. After realizing what he was up against his realization for the need of this employment was greater. He was determined to feed his family and make better provision for them. He was not willing to be intimidated because of what he did not have. His tenacity in what he possessed seemed to be enough to get the job done. His desire to obtain a better way of life for his family caused him to pursue his happiness. Truly, he was indifferent from those that had all the right requirements, but he claimed it. You must believe what is meant for you is for you. Commit to that in your mind and go get your new life. It is out there waiting for you! Every step you take *matters because there is wisdom to gain and cause you to be prosperous. Never let a step you take be taken for granted, rather be a learning tool to become a great and wiser you.*

The Process

The process could be more timely than expected and it is up to how well you anticipate your development. Process is the method for progression. Before you can progress you must administer the right mindset for development. Your course of action determines your outcome in life. The sooner you are willing to follow the right procedures to obtain what you need for purpose fulfillment in your life, the more rapidly you can become a wealthier inhibitor. Not speaking of money, but happiness. Get on the right course to fulfill your purpose.

It's Time You Make A Change To Become A Better You!

There is only one path and it is the right one. Notice when people see their favorite stars or someone that is more fortunate, how they react. Truly, they do not know what they endured to obtain their position in life. It was not easy for the ones that literally had to work for it or inherited it. Someone paid the price. Yes, inheritance is not easy if your loved ones had to lose their life for you to gain. Wealth is not money, rather the pursuit of your peace and happiness. I have noticed pursuing happiness is very painful and causes a lot of grief. Yes, you must fight for your peace. Nevertheless, you have to develop to be processed because it will not stop until you advance. Proper development is purposed to cultivate the way you think and to create a way for you to obtain those things in your heart. Momentarily, once you foster a new perception of life you will have the power to acquire one.

The New You Is Pending

One day I looked in the mirror and cried my heart out. Afterwards I felt so empty. I questioned God, "Why do you require so much of me?" He answered, "It's not hard and if I did not think you would complete the tasks I would not have given them to you?" I also cried to Him and told Him, "I have been waiting on you." His response, "I have been waiting on you too." Immediately I laughed because all the time I am waiting He has been too. I realized whatever I was doing in this season He was going to contribute to my effort. I wait, He waits. I work and He works. I go forth He multiplies. That was the most productive cry I have ever done in my life because I realized that I was holding up my own prosperity. Is this you?

Once you notice the questions you are asking in your spirit then you too will realize. A call out for help deserves a responsive answer. Let your tears cause you to increase in wisdom and bring out the best in you.

Life Changing Inspirations

It is good to inspire because you are encouraging someone to thrive in life. There is something inside you worth digging for. My daughter wrote an inspiring paper to obtain a college scholarship. She said, "Mom, you are my inspiration." She was one of the four candidates awarded the scholarship. Also, I knew another young lady that was one of my previous clients from childhood. The effect I had in her life was inspiring. She was always calm and quite. However, she was paying me a lot of attention. She too wrote a paper inquiring about a college scholarship and I was a part of her inspiration. She and my daughter have something in common, tenacity and a determined minds to pursue their happiness. You will be surprised how your life will impact others. Your life means something to someone whether you realize it or not. You are impacting someone to take another route in life.

After my daughter went to college she too returned the inspiration. No one knows what my family endured, but, we do and nothing stops those who are purposed to win. I mean absolutely nothing. How ambitious are

It's Time You Make A Change To Become A Better You!

you? Through my years plenty inspired me. In order to inspiring others you have to have the ear to hear and the heart to motivate. My heart's desire is to motivate all to live limitless in their happiness!

It's Time You Make A Change To Become A Better You!

From **Eating Crumbs to Transforming WEALTH**

Chapter Six
Cultivate Your Ground

Maybe you have wanted your breakthrough of wealth; however, it still has not happened. Perhaps, money cannot buy your happiness or supply your needs. I realized poor and rich people have something in common that money cannot buy, and that is the pursuit of their happiness. We all cry and feel the pains of life the same. Transformation of the comfortable place dwells deep within you. Happiness within is a place that has not yet found neither defined. It is treasured with pure fulfillment. It has not come in the mail, transferred to your bank account or placed on your doorstep. You have been looking for it desperately, and you want it now! You have to crank up your search because your life depends on this transformation. You are expecting but have not put forth the right determination. If so, it would be evident! Your wealthy place can only inherit from within you. A life transformation is a way of reforming the way you think and the tactics you use. It is something you still have not tapped into that is keeping your destiny hidden. I once was registering my son for school, and I was explaining to the registrar that my son is a gifted child. He is frequently in honors classes. He looked into my son's eyes and said, "If you are in honors the best advice I can give you is prove it." You cannot do the same thing and expect new or good results. The time is now to change the way you have been pursuing life. It is the time you make a change in the way you handle business and prove yourself. To become someone you never have, you have to take steps you have never made. The change is inside you, but the proof is in your plan to succeed.

Little Change Is Big Power

If it is hard for you to make a little change, then big will overwhelm you. For an example, a little habit requires a determined mind to stop. Is your effort not enough to make this change? The effort is your trying ability, but in some cases trying is not enough. If success is not your result then what good was your effort? However, your exertion is what you need to go beyond the effort to make real progress. It seems little to you, but it is huge to others. Challenge yourself to throw that habit away.

The more you move forward without going backward, the further forward you will get. One of my greatest challenges was smoking cigarettes. It was a small thing that I loved doing, yet a bad habit I needed to quit. It consumed the breath of many I was around as I smoked. I made some people cough, and then others choked. Often I saw people fan, and I still smoked. All those years my children suffered the abuse of mom being a smoker. My bad habit caused many to be uncomfortable. No matter how good you appear to people when they see your bad habits, it also affects how you are viewed. Exchange your bad habits for a better you because it affects many.

After a while, I stopped smoking in the house and cars so I would not smoke around the children. Second-hand smoke is worse than first-hand smoke. As I quit, I also stopped contributing to air pollution. One day I realized what was more important to my family a smoke-free car, house or mom? Transformation is more than self it is the happiness of a union of productivity. Seeking the respect of others always causes real life changes. Cultivating your ground to be respectful is the best change you can make. Allow others to view a good and respectful character in you that will always cause a better you to be produced.

It's Time You Make A Change To Become A Better You!

I stopped at a rest area once as we were traveling. I saw this beautiful navy blue Bentley, and it looked like it just comes from a showroom exhibit. Standing near was this older gentleman taking a cigarette break, and his smile seemed so natural. As I was passing by we greeted one another, and I said, "Nice car." He replied, "My wife brought it for me, and she doesn't want me to smoke in it." I said, "WOW"! Sir, you'd rather smoke up the only living body you will ever get and cannot replace it?" He looked with his embroidered smile, and I tried to encourage him to spare the body because life is worth more than a car. He laughed and said, "You sound like my wife." However, he kept on smoking. I hope he has quit by now because he seemed to be a fun and good gentlemen. One bad habit has life-

long effects on the ones you love and are dear to you. It is the simple little bad habits that can cause massive change, and sooner or later we all feel the raft of calamity as an after effect. A sure way to appreciate the pursuit of your happiness is to be able to enjoy the fruit of your labor.

Big change with Big Mindset

Once you begin to prove to yourself that you can handle the little changes, then you are ready for progress. It is the small change that shows you can handle big changes. The little is the preparation for growth and growth is the proof development of a better life. Mature development brings forth good results once one can handle growth. It is impossible to begin in middle school if you have never completed ele-

mentary. *Your little change is vital to be able to handle significant advancement. You must prove you can handle small things and small tasks before trust with greater challenges. Movement requires steps forward to establish growth. Once the way you think graduates from your rational thinking mode, then your life will be upgraded. You will make great and good progress with completing small tasks first.*

Plowing Intentionally

You can have the right intentions with the erratic movement. The right things plus the right strategies will orchestrate the right outcome. Are you causing your children to eat the crumbs of your life or causing them to endeavor? Crumbs are never satisfying, and they always keep you in a hungered state. It is not good for the mind to continuously hunger for a lot of needs and not enough satisfaction. Are you causing your children or ones that believe in you to become more than a conqueror through your inspiring effort? Improve your life it will make it easier for them and you to live.

Children hurt, and they get overwhelmed with the pressures of life too. If you are reading this book, it is not too late to transform your mind. If you transform the way, you think you can change your life. Digging in search of the improved you is worth the fighting effort. Continue to plow and dig deeper to find your life transformation it will be worth the sweat.

It's Time You Make A Change To Become A Better You!

Real Results Are Worth Every Effort

Dig deeper for a better you. Your power is in the depth of your madness to succeed and receive your life transformation. Your passion to strive will cause an explosive outcome in pursuing your happiness to reach your place of wealth. It is the time you prove to yourself that you changed. Once you begin to see results, then you are changed. Noticing change gets results! If you cannot see change, then it does not exist. Some people try to fake their change; however, your life shows the picture of who you are. Change is viewable, and it is a landscape of your life. A positive change always produces good results and defines right increase as your outcome. It is the result of your words put into action.

It's Time You Make A Change To Become A Better You!

From **Eating Crumbs to Transforming WEALTH**

Chapter Seven
Sweat & Get Results

There Are some treasures inside you to ripen your future, improve your lifestyle and advance your family. The question is, "Are they worth digging for?" In that comfortable place is the identity; the reason you was created. Once you connect with the treasure inside, then the wealth will be transferred to your next generation. It is sweating time. The more your children see you sweat to get real results the better you will empower them to reach big. Seeds only produce after its kind. If you notice them not being productive, then examine yourself. If they see your progress, then it will be easier for them to accomplish. Fighting for your next generation is worth the sweat. Once one begins to experience the sweat on a consistent basis eventually, they obtain real results.

A Refining Moment

An improving moment identifies what kind of person you are. Once you open your eyes and take a deep look and then a self-inventory of your product, you have been examined. You are a product whether you realize it or not. Are your goods producing what you need? It may sound strange, but if you have an idea, vision, or business, then you are a product.

It's Time You Make A Change To Become A Better You!

Think about when you go shopping. Looking at all the stores, you know exactly what you are going to purchase. Is your product worth investing in, worth purchasing or taking the time to look at? WOW! Notice, what kind of person you are. Your neighborhood, clothes, personality, character, and attitude are representing how well others view you. If anything about you seems out of place or incorrect, then it is time to make that change. If your business sales are down, then it is time to make a change. Only you have that power to make it happen and your motivation power fuels your determination. So how much will you invest into your empowering? This is not the time to get upset or depressed; rather, it is your time to get real results!

Empowerment Hour

It's Time You Make A Change To Become A Better You!

Yes, your empowerment will make you determined! So many people waste valuable time because they are not motivated enough to be productive. A lot of people will give every excuse in the book not to make a change allowing their negatives to overpower them. I continuously ask myself this question, "What kind of person are you?" The key to creation is that it is never completed. So many think once they accomplish a good thing or goal they are finished. No, it is still the beginning! Creation never stops it continues to cause more vision. A Fine example of production continuing would be as one person makes up their mind to lose a certain amount of weight to appear attractive and healthy. Once many people reach their goal, they stop exercising and go back to their bad eating habits. The key is a continuous ef-

fort to keeping the good habits alive. Once a goal is accomplished, do not quit. Continue with the adoption of change that caused you to obtain good results. The exact mindset you implemented to achieve the goal is the same, plus new mindset is needed to continue seeing good results. Meditation of good thinking will inhabit really good results because it nourishes the mind. That is why preparation is more important than the end results. The more time you put in preparing yourself for a particular task, the better your results are going to be. I love to use Michael Jackson for an example. He was an extraordinary performer. No, he did not make it overnight but through many years of hardcore practice and dripping sweat. I do believe he continuously strived for perfection even his best was not good enough

It's Time You Make A Change To Become A Better You!

because he always strived to do better. Whatever you have previously tried to accomplish and feel you have failed at, try it again; do it better. Work harder toward a goal of perfection. There is no power of good results in one that quits. To set aside an hour of empowerment to feed your mind, good thinking habits are needed to invest in your motivation. It is a plus to achieve greater accomplishments and conquering power!

Lack of Motivation Equals No Pushing Power

Motivation is the key because it fuels you to push. One way I do my hour of empowerment is walking with a word. The more I walk, the more I get revelation on the main points of the scriptures. I recite as I walk. Yes, there are times I am not meditating as I should; then I become less productive. I begin to feel faint, tired and weak. Also, I begin to put on more weight. Besides, when I feed my active mind empowerment, I accomplish so much more. I enhance my writing skills and speaking ability. My home is more inspired and when I meet people I am represented well because my spirit is upbeat. I also attend motivational workshops and listen to great motivational speakers that inspire me. My advice to you is to invest in your motivation. It can be conferences, books, empowerment sessions, music or audio. As long as you stay motivated you will have the fuel to go places you have never been and accomplish goals you never thought would come to pass. Never think your inspiration is not worth the price. If you need motiva-

tion invest in things that inspire you to be ready because a serious state of mind always needs a mighty push!

Creating Time for Good Thinking

Time is an essential point to opportunity! So many pass opportunity for an increase every second of the day until it turns into years of no progress. It is true. Transformation can only exist after the change occurs. No change, no transformation, and your happiness are worth pursuing. How, can someone obtain something they have not worked hard? Two ways to obtain inheritance: theft or your hot sweat. It is necessary and vital to set aside time to motivate good thinking habits. Good thinkers are more guaranteed to be successful than negative thinkers. A sure way to make *time is set your alarm clock a few minutes earlier. There are too many ways to list lunch, dinner, break and so on. There is no excuse not to be successful. There are 24 hours in a day, seven days a week, which equals 168 hours tallying, about 672 monthly hours to get results. Think about how much time you have wasted. Time is irreplaceable! You would be surprised how 15 minutes a day of empowerment could inspire you. Also, adding 15 minutes of creation with your effort can produce. Replacing a few commercials, a ride to the store, a 15-minute break or a phone conversation just a few days a week can get you good end results.*

Your Happiness is Worth the Time

Your happiness is worth making time to pursue because it is your joy. The more positive results you achieve, the more powerful you will become. Always remain teachable so that you can be reachable. Regardless of the outcome, never stop creating a better way because as time changes you need to also. If you allow your goods to grow old, then you become outdated. Notice in stores, old items are passed on and removed from the shelves. Always stay revealing and fresh so that you will have a domino effect. Dominos always get the attention of the eye and showcase products always obtain more sales. So whatever your idea, vision or business make sure it is causing a good effect and stay marketable. A good product will always be worth ordering. Once you become "out of stock", at one location it makes room for others to request your product, business or vision. Are you staying mar-

ketable is the question you need to ask daily yourself? You need definite, detailed goals and a higher power to recognize the full potential that is inside of you! Remember, your happiness is worth the serious effort to pursue and never accept no for an answer. Utilize the "no's" in your life for your new push.

It's Time You Make A Change To Become A Better You!

From **Eating Crumbs to Transforming WEALTH**

Chapter Eight
Running Power

A Thought For You:

Have you ever been a contestant but running in the wrong race. Once I was running a race but I was in the wrong city, the wrong place at the wrong time.

Your spiritual trainer matters. You have to know how to use what you have. If something is working incorrectly, then there is a problem. It is alright to clarify something to obtain the right information. To push whatever is in you out. You must have pushing power because if you don't you will be in *plenty of pain. There is only one way to stop the birthing pains of your vision; you must push until it comes out. Quiet noticeably the pains come again because simply what's growing inside is stretching you and there is no more room for growth.*

Spiritual leaders are imperative because they have your guide to heaven, prosperity, salvation, the road to destiny, faith, praying power and so much more. Generally speaking, they are your spiritual trainer and so are ones that you associate closely. So, therefore, you need to know them in the spirit, not just by looks and stuff. The key factor is your leader causing you to stretch, to have more faith and to be more developed? Indeed, many are called, but few are chosen. I have met people that will quote a word but have no value or power. Simply meaning anyone can read a word but how many can be a word? To get spiritually fit you need to hire the best spiritual trainer that can get the job done because time is a terrible thing to waste. Contractions are always painful. The more the pain the harder the labor and your labor requires more pushing power. For this birth through you, that is about to take place just remember much is given, and much more is needed. If you want the birthing pains to stop, push with power!

The WORD in is your reproduction and multiplication as long as you have the right revelation. It teaches you and gets you spiritually fit for the journey that is bigger than you. The WORD is your manifestation and your food for all your life equations. I love to praise God especially when I'm going to

It's Time You Make A Change To Become A Better You!

feast on a Good Healthy WORD. The right WORD will gas you, and the fuel won't run out because you will know when it is time to fill back up. It will carry you with reserve. The WORD gives you the right nutrients for good nourishment, and it always replenishes because it is healthy for your soul and household. In the WORD are hidden treasures, and that will lead you to valuable artifacts which are enrichment tools for your vision as well as gifts. It also nourishes which is malnourished. The WORD has many secret compartments that the world cannot comprehend to keep the values hidden. In those values is concealed peace and suppressed goods that an ordinary thinker can't understand. Peace surpasses all understanding, but it's in the WORD. Some try to perform in action as they have the WORD or pretend but soon their performance will bore you. However, you must obtain the right revelation to get the right transformation. Many false leaders are called sanctimonious praise and worship. It is contaminating the ones that trust the people and not the WORD. It is built on pretense but cannot convert. If leaders are not aligned or aligning up to the WORD, then they are called and not chosen. The Chosen will change because they will not be able to continue being themselves. Many signs will be shown through them that will possess the fruit of the spirit because of their secret compartments of factored viewpoints. I am pushing, but nothing is happening. If you have not seen it yet, it's coming!

Tapping Into Your New Strengths

It's Time You Make A Change To Become A Better You!

So many people think they have what it takes to make something happen, but they don't. There are so many things you must get to make stuff happen. A whole new you! Yes, it sounds crazy, but it is true. To accomplish something you never had you must become someone you have never been! James 4:7 speaks of resisting the devil and he will flee. The devil is purposed to tempt you to get weak so that your future of prosperity will be held back. The temptation is allowing your flesh, and enticing it to feel, and emotions, not healthy pleasures. However, in this scripture, James want you to see the concepts of deception. If you resist temptations, you tap into a strength which resists. The more you resist, the stronger you become. Resistance is muscle power to allow a new force to take over. Once you grow stronger by recognizing you are – not – to remain your sight will become clearer. You will also be strengthened even in your viewpoints because what used to be out of sight will be placed in your view.

There is Power in No

The more you say no, the more He can say yes. There is more power than you realize in your no but you will never know until you begin to say no. Once you act upon and stand on your no then that temptation will not be able to stir up desires that cause you to appear puny. I will never forget when I quit smoking. James 4:7 was my help. I continued to speak James 4:7 every time temptation tried to arouse me. I no longer want to look like a pathetic minister or appear fragile. The more I confessed it, the more I withdrew from smoking. I just took one day at a time and kept moving far away. I begin that fight in September 2006, and soon afterward I overcame. Life is something how we allow simple little things to keep us in bondage and away from so many beautiful things. I realized if I was going to accomplish big then I must grow big in faith and my faith needed strength it never had. Yes, the power in our no is the assurance of our faith! It also helped my faith to be able to stretch. Also, I realize how good a yes sounds after receiving so many no's.

Elastic Faith

Anytime you need to do exceedingly above all you have ever done you need a clear vision.

It's Time You Make A Change To Become A Better You!

Often many try to accomplish something impossible, and their faith is not currently at that level of all possible. It won't work. Faith is not to stay the same size or shape. A fine example of faith is like elastic it needs to be stretchable when purposed to be strong. Faith is simply limitless possibilities at all times. It must build and then be exercised. The greatest failure of faith is when one runs before time then calamity comes. Faith is something that stretches in the biggest time of need, and it's wearable though any season plus condition. It has no conditions, and it can handle all situations. It has no extreme of limits it just goes to work when one believes. Yes, it is stretchable - one size fits all! But, can you handle to ride faith as far as it will take you? Some could not treat religion as their eyes saw more than their faith could feel they turned back or stopped believing. Notice, faith cannot go to work if you are not willing to exercise your belief. Your belief causes faith to show up and show out. Doubt and fear will cancel out faith when one is not being strengthened to believe greater. I am pushing, but nothing is happening. If you have not seen it yet, it's coming!

Resistant is the power you need to build muscle in tired and weak areas of your belief. Yes, no simply makes you stronger than you can stretch as elastic becoming expandable. Resisting temptation causes you to be challenged in the area you're feeble. You cannot get an expansion until you grow large. It's time to increase your flexibility. Elastic is a stretching with comfort and adapting to change. It builds our confidence.

Compete for Power

Race needs contestants and without competitors, there is no competition. Nothing to compete for requires no race and no race no winners. Race is set for rivals to participate not in strength but endurance to achieve the many challenges ahead. It prepares one to be great in sportsmanship. Just as one appears to be a runner by looking fit, being smart, strong and so on, the real truth will be at the finish line. A contestant may look qualified but are not fit but for a mile. Others may seem well educated, but their smarts may not have an enduring power to complete the assignment. Also, some may have a proven background to *be a great contestant with a great track record but still out of shape for this race. One day I laughed because I was doing the right things, with the right moves, making the right decisions but in the wrong place. I thought I was in the right race. Surely, I was running but in the wrong state. Notice your competitors also help to strengthen your running power. What good is a race without competitors? Competitors are happy to have their challenge you to be a winner if you stay focused on winning. Ecclesiastes 9:11 reminds us it is more than strength, wisdom, swiftness, food, riches, or skill but the opportunity to conquer is for all. Nevertheless, stay prepared to be ready when your chance comes. It's coming, just be prepared!*

It's Time You Make A Change To Become A Better You!

From **Eating Crumbs to Transforming WEALTH**

Powerful Inspiring books by Parice Parker

Living Life in A Messed Up Situation

Volume One

Living Life in A Messed Up Situation

Volume Two

Power to Push You

A Precious Gift from God

Word Wonders

The Anointing Powers of Your Hands

From Eating Crumbs to Transforming Wealth

The Birth of an Author Shall Be Born

Live Love Laugh & Be Happy

Aggravated Assault On Your Mind

The Revised Edition

Visit Our Online Book Store or Where Ever Books Are Sold

www.pariceparker.biz

Change Your Company – Change Your Season.

It's Time You Make A Change To Become A Better You!

Aggravated Assault on Your Mind

Have you ever felt, the very person you have surely loved or believed in has attacked you? It may have been your closest friend, relative, child, your spouse or even yourself. Sometimes you wanted to cry and could not. Shortly afterwards, while gazing about the pain immediately tears began to fall as a flowing river. Your heart has been assaulted and snared with claws of intentions to kill. A multitude of thoughts circulate in your mind and then you began to say to

It's Time You Make A Change To Become A Better You!

yourself **"How did I let this happen to me?"** Your situation was bound to occur, because somewhere along the way you have allowed your circumstance to control your mind. Allegedly, you put your trust in the wrong one or thing and then you are thrown off guard. Most definitely, you wonder, who do I blame? You did not realize you have entrusted so much of your heart to be assaulted through the passion of love you have given. A since of blindness has overwhelmed your thinking ability, rearranging your life, and throwing it off balance. Truly, there is an explanation and an apology due, but none is ever given. Certainly, you have tried to generate an effectual change. Perhaps, the more you have tried, the more your relationship seemed to die. **Instantly thinking, What Is The Use?**

It's Time You Make A Change To Become A Better You!

A Precious Gift from God

Your Gift Discovery? It teaches one the value of their natural born talent and motivates one to Live Life On Purpose! This book inspires the heart, gives courage to your *How to Ability* and causes you to live in the pursuit of your happiness. Every natural born leader needs to read this book, it is **AWE – INSPIRING!**

It's Time You Make A Change To Become A Better You!

Living Life In A Messed Up Situation
Volume One

God will assign the most in-depth spiritual cleaning service through the Blood of Jesus the Christ to clean up your messed up life. **Every messed up situation that you are living** in will have a **Sparkling Effect** when God gets finished with you. Some things He dusts off, others He wipes down and some need to be polished to shine. **Get Polished Perfect** after reading this book and simply gain it all.

It's Time You Make A Change To Become A Better You!

Living Life In A Messed Up Situation
Volume Two

Astounding ... It seems though many things has changed within your life including your perseverance. Often you wanted to quit but couldn't afford to even STOP TRYING! As life twirled down so did your hope, dreams and prosperity. Order this book today and Reel In Your Greatest CATCH! A Mega Booster is what you need and this is it! Let JESUS catch You Trying!

It's Time You Make A Change To Become A Better You!

The Birth of An Author Shall Be Born

Fascinating ... Dazing at the fact you have a book inside and don't know where to start or how to get it out! This book have dynamic key points and great strategies on how to succeed in book writing from start to finish. It's time to discover the author in you and to **GET THAT BOOK OUT Of YOU!** This book is full of techniques to motivate the author inside... The Birth of an Author Shall Be Born, Is It YOU?

It's Time You Make A Change To Become A Better You!

Word Wonders

A Eye – Opening ... Word Wonder inspires your HOPE to Greatly Influence your FAITH and it's a magnificent daily devotional book to help keep you focused in word. It EMPOWERS Positive Powers to cause DIVINE FAVOR to ABOUND TOWARDS YOU! Simple things you need to be equipped with more favor from on high. Get This Book TODAY!

It's Time You Make A Change To Become A Better You!

From Eating Crumbs To Transforming Wealth

Riveting ... Finally, a book that keeps you in a thriving mental state that causes your HOPE to burst through! Now, it is time to identify the real you by introducing the TROPHY that is Hidden inside. It's your time to stop eating the crumbs of life and Indulge In Your WEALTHY Place!

It's Time You Make A Change To Become A Better You!

Live Love Laugh & Be Happy

Live Love
Laugh
&
Be
Happy

It's like medicine to your bones ...
Parice Parker

Live Love Laugh & Be Happy *Fabulous* ... Daily many live life being terribly unhappy wanting others to really care but, are too often overlooked. It's time you get a new ray of hope. A time for healing inside and out. Live Love Laugh & Be Happy is purposed to expose new life to your everyday living. Your laughter is on its way, because those that sow in tears of sorrow, shall reap in tears of joy!

125   Change Your Company – Change Your Season.

It's Time You Make A Change To Become A Better You!

Power to Push You

Militant Force ... When you fix your mind on the power to excel and purpose to hit the target, then it is a done deal. Your goal is now to achieve. No one, nothing or tiredness could stop you now. Power to Push You is missioned to cause you to be an eye specialist. Your eyes will begin to see the benefits of vision; the aspirations once accomplished, and you will have an IMPETUOUS ZEAL. No one can dream for this vision as you or push it in the manner you can and stay focused as you. Vision is the power to drive people but first

It's Time You Make A Change To Become A Better You!

one must see the fullness, must feel the passion for it to live and have an IMPETUOUS ZEAL to birth it.

Vision is a life modifier and life decorator. It can give you a complete makeover from inside out. Also, when others see it, they will want to be a part or some of what you have. Your success will cause others to desire a much better life and give others a fresh hope to accomplish. Power to Push You speaks for itself and all that connects and read Power to Push You shall cause their visions to exist. It's a DYNOMITE PUSHER!

It's Time You Make A Change To Become A Better You!

Fountain of Life Publisher's House

www.pariceparker.biz

It's Time You Make A Change To Become A Better You!

From **Eating Crumbs to Transforming WEALTH**

If evidence is not your end result then what good is your effort?
~ Parice Parker

<u>It's Time You Make A Change To Become A Better You!</u>

Thanks You So Much & Be Blessed!

It's Time You Make A Change To Become A Better You!

www.ingramcontent.com/pod-product-compliance
Lightning Source LLC
Chambersburg PA
CBHW070556160426
43199CB00014B/2524